A Cartography of Home

Also by Hayden Saunier

How to Wear This Body
Say Luck
Tips for Domestic Travel

Field Trip to the Underworld (chapbook)

A Cartography of Home

by

Hayden Saunier

Terrapin Books

Terrapin Books
4 Midvale Avenue
West Caldwell, NJ 07006

www.terrapinbooks.com

ISBN: 978-1-947896-35-2
Library of Congress Control Number: 2020941413

First Edition

Cover art by Hayden Saunier

for R.E.B.

Contents

Where you come from is gone, where you thought you were going to was never there, and where you are is no good...In yourself right now is all the place you've got.
—Flannery O'Connor

Places matter...They map our lives.
—Rebecca Solnit

1

Kitchen Table

Our kitchen table's made of walls.
Wide planks that sheathed clapboard, salvaged
from the sagging side of the house

we pulled down, boards spared from dry rot,
sanded smooth by our hands.
Our table's made of walls that held

a family of six before typhoid took
both parents and fostered out the children
to farm families needing help. Our table's

made of old growth forests no longer forests
but fields that offer stone and sinew,
antler, bone, tin cans, bottles, blades,

each spring a brand new crop of everything
that's come before. Our table's wood
is spalted through with hard luck, grease,

disease, fat streaks of amber jam.
Our table's made of all of it.
It's us and ours. Sit down and eat.

Liminal

Liquid green-gold gathers outside
the window frame, lightens with a swelling pulse.

First world
        or memory of first world—
        no difference.

Close your eyes.
Here is the moment before
        leaves unfurl, each edge

        articulating fiddlehead
        or fan or elephant ear

before a mot-mot sings in a mango tree
or a house wren chatters in an oak

        and you remember
precisely where you are.

But for now, there's no telling
what's inside,
        what's out.

Only how most mornings it's there.

Everything you knew
before you knew anything.

I'm Also the Fox

The day starts with a green cardboard quart
of under-ripened, overfed strawberries sliced

with a worn-down knife, berries snipped
long before each pixie cap could part from the fruit

it fed with the soft plosive of a blown kiss,
whose seed-flecked flesh never stood a chance,

crated and trucked over drought-dried rivers
and continental divides because we are divided

from our food in the way we are divided from
each other and divided from ourselves, so I say

good morning, sad berries, as I stand at the sink
slicing their bitterness into smaller bits of bitterness

that I'll feed to chickens, slicing hard white parts
and bruised gray parts because having no chance

from the get-go can be rotted and unripe both.
My chickens will love this wildly out-of-season flesh.

Even though studded with gritty seeds soaked
in pesticides and sliced while I wait as their eggs

hard boil on the stove. It's a small bargain I make.
I have time to bargain, you see, my pantry

is full, no one pounds down my door, no drones
overhead, no rubble needs to be cleared from the road

into town, the town still stands, there's water here,
it's clean. I have time to slice small bitterness smaller,

to disappear it into something else, time to study
the knife's worn blade, thin crescent of steel so dull

I cut against the pad of my thumb without fear.
Knife handed down with sink, stone farmhouse,

pantry, tractor, bank stock, safety, skin. Pretense
of balance, bucolic calm, soft slushing of slices,

eggs rumbling against the saucepan's solid wall.
By day's end, the chickens will shit out the berries

I've sliced, three hens will be taken by fox, another
by hawk, their bright checkered feathers strewn up

the creek bed, blood spotting the rocks, their eggs
cold in rows in the icebox. Tonight, from wood's edge,

from the darkening rooms of my house, I'll answer
the gaze of that fox with my gaze. She'll turn back

into forest, I'll step back into stone. Above us,
hickories and pin oaks will shoulder each other for sky.

Dirt Smart

You have to eat a peck of dirt
before you die, my grandma said.
I worried. Do I *have* to?
Is that required? Or is a peck the breaking point
and *then* you die? What *is* a peck?
She grew up surrounded by small plots
of clean red dirt, no sidewalks or storefronts,
just golden burley and bright leaf
tobacco fields dug deep with labor, slaughter
and someone's finger weighting every scale,
the way most land accumulation's won.
In school I knew a kid who ate dirt
before anyone even made him.
When I asked my grandma why
I learned what hunger bullies
souls to do. She knew the dirt
you ate, the dirt beneath your fingernails,
dirt scrubbed from palm and kneecap
with cold water and a bristle brush—
that's all the earth you own.
It's not what kills you either.

Speech

First thing, first light, I step barefooted
on the small hard skull of a bodiless

mouse, which sparks a surge of neural
dance steps up my legs and yes,

I expect this from a life that includes cats,
who teach me that every night

I curl up with killers, every day
I walk over the dead, and no, I can't

count the layers of the once-living
stacked beneath me. I only know

how each dead thing delivers the same
brief, motivational speech directly

to my spine, whether or not their
small bones quick-dance through my feet.

Cold Morning with New Catastrophes

Crickets stopped scratching their names
in last evening's dark husk,
the false summer over as half of the earth

lurched sudden and blind into winter.
Then terrible noises all night.
Coyotes, for certain, fierce hunger

on fast compact paws, but also
the singular cries of their prey
as the hinge between seasons gave way,

unshuttered the bright
broken cold of this day.
Still, those terrible sounds in the night.

Some I heard; most were too far away.
No switch to turn off what's caught in the ear,
in the wind, no naming this dread

just the gift of more light to see
so much cold. Even the comforting slap
of my black rubber boots

snapping back on my calves
seems a clock counting down,
as I walk to the still-flowing creek,

that may well be poisoned,
or maybe not poisoned, or maybe,
this morning, not yet.

Morning Drift

I wake in a small house with one blue wall
by a cold sea, also blue,

        most days transparent
where water works itself thin at the edges,

the door of the house open
        to the hammering of men

        bending wood into boats
which is the sound of anger

framed as buoyancy and shaped
like cupped hands

        that hold, but not much
        and not long.

Here the beach is called shingle.
As if flat stones make a roof

        I could balance on.

They keep their names to themselves,
the many shy birds

I don't see watching me
        lie down on the pitch of the earth.

It's magic, how after looking at blue,
my closed eyes see red.

> Magic, too, how each morning
> you come alive and stay alive

until the cold moment
> I remember you're not.

Locks

Ghosts have a way of knowing where all the keys are hidden.
—William Evans

As though we, the living, are locks.
Or doors with locks.

Or small latched boxes,
lacquered or decoupaged with pansies,

or scorched like the unpainted dime store kind
you tried to inscribe with your name

with a neighbor kid's wood burning kit,
all of them with a tiny hasp

and padlock worked by a thin gold key
that even a ghost could lose.

As though there are ghosts, real ones,
not simply regret.

As though regret were simple.
As though it were made complicated only

by our intricate tricks for containing
the ghosts of what we can't let go,

but grieve and grieve and grieve over,
as though we were not the lock,

the latch, the lid, the door, not the rue,
not the sorrow, not the ghost with the key.

Inhabitant

Whoever you were,
you lived
in the rooms,
rinsed the cup, dried the plate,

slept & wept & swept
the same three wooden steps.

Each spring, like me,
you saw storms clean
the sheltering trees
of superfluity—

what holds tight
still lives,
what lives, stays aloft.

Today, I lift
from the shaken-down scatter,
an oriole's intricate
basketry nest,

blue twine
woven through it
for structure,

your hair spun
in swirls for a bed.
As, someday, I know,
so will mine.

Forecast

Halfway through August,
      summer cracks

and shatters into thick clay shards
pieced quickly back together
      with the sticky glue
of more hot days

      but no one's fooled.

Something swift
      and slender crosses the path.

Let's pretend
it's only animal, not sign.

2

A Brief Inventory of Now

Mad fury all around.
Yesterday's blown curtains of cold rain
thrash a far-off coastline, leave behind a world

of wind and wind's demand
for kowtow, scrape and bow, the meadow
grasses flattened, trees bent down, small birds

flung about like comedy
gone cruel. Inside, an upturned cup and its
attendant spoon dry on a tea towel's smooth

blue surface, serene as a dory
with a single oar beached above
the tide line in a scene flown in from some

distant time and place.
Even now, memory insists on taking space.
Gusts throw chaff against each solitary pane

of glass. It's possible this house
won't hold. Inside, scrabble of pounce and claw
across the kitchen floor as two cats team up

to corner a mouse. Tails twitch.
Wind raises its pitch. This could go
either way, any moment, and no telling which.

That Summer

Everyone was curating something.
Baby doll heads found in the river,

eyeless or one-eyed or blue-eyed
with ragged black lashes; deer

jawbones pulled from the gullies
where antlers were sawed from their skulls

in the fall; social media pages; the news.
For weeks, it was terribly hot.

Slender women in bias-cut dresses
reported the heat, how it felt, every hour.

Surfaces burned. We cataloged and culled
what gathered around us, laid out

collections on white butcher paper,
concocted new stories to make things

make sense, but still, we forgot to remember
that *curator* means someone who cares.

After the Press Conference

I'm back outside, hands deep in dirt and dirt's
the only thing that's telling truth today.
O.K. I overstate. Dirt's not the only thing
that's telling truth. My hands, in fact, aren't in
the dirt—I'm wearing gloves, the woven fabric
kind coated in synthetic rubber polymers
which is the truth because I looked it up
and took that definition from two independent
scientific sources, but it's not a truth I know
the way I know how to wrench and cleave
a plant into pieces with a sharp spade,
garden fork, and fixed knife blade.
We call this *propagation by division.*
I loosen roots with my gloved hands, dirt
being all that holds their threads together.
Dirt: from, or cognate with, a half dozen
Middle English, Old Dutch, Proto-Indo-European,
and Norwegian words for excrement.
This dirt is mid-Atlantic farm dirt flecked
with mica, shale, leaf mold, fungi, and the shit
of four Sicilian donkeys and a Shetland pony.
Truth is we know when someone's lying.
Truth is we know when we pretend we don't know
someone's lying, when we let the lie go, take the money.
This dirt's not telling truth, it isn't saying anything.
Except: *this shit's not complicated* and: *we're in it now.*

What We Make Looks Just Like Us

A pair of brass fox faces
fashioned on an ornate pair of andirons

stare out dead-eyed from the gleaming
blackened hearth

as if pretense and unshaken
belief in cleverness could mean

the blazing stack of logs aflame
across their backs is not

a blazing stack of logs aflame
across their backs

as long as they pretend it's not.
It burns and burns and they don't even blink.

Solo Act

A single oak leaf
on the toe shoe
of its needle tip
turned perfect
solitary pirouettes
on an empty
blacktopped road
in a performance
designed for no one
but witnessed
by me and a steep
grandstand full
of condemned trees
making the sound
of applause
but that turned out
to be simply
the sound made
by trees when
pink tags flutter
in the smallest breeze.

Confirmation Bias at the Minimarket

My friend whispers that the minimarket clerk has been eating
    too long the pulverized flesh of mistreated
        chickens raised on Roundup-Ready
genetically modified corn-based
    poultry chow that would account
        for her dead eyes & eyes dead
    of anything but the lethal stare she sports

as if years of built-up resentments
    held tight in the segmented stems of flora
        & brainstems of fauna
are screaming on a cellular level through this minimarket clerk
    & she's not doing her level best
        to hold the animus back
    but I tell my friend

I've done that job & it's not food it's pay
    & fear & what's there & not there
        wherever the minimarket clerk
calls home & I want to say to the minimarket clerk
    I've been there
        because I've been there
    but because I've been there

I don't think she wants to hear that I've been there
    from me or anyone else
        when she's still there
and I am not & besides my friend's behaving
    like a walking example of organic

food privilege
from a small college town

& for godssakes we're here buying water & my friend
is looking for something gluten-free
for no real reason so we pay &
leave & I turn around & say I'm sorry
so sorry & thank you, we're idiots, forgive us—
no, don't—we are exactly
who and what you thought when we walked in.
That's when she smiles.

Insomnia in a Highway Motel

Truck commerce, relentless
downshift, upshift, 3 a.m.
gear catch and shudder
and someone somewhere
standing on a floodlit loading dock
is counting on each manifest.
I'm counting tire-ticks clicking
over tar expansion joints.
Lubdub. Lubdub. In the dark
cavern between eyelid and eye,
I construct this dumbass hope
that what is being freighted
through the night resolves
with daylight into burlap sacks
of rice and barley, tangerines,
blankets, vials of insulin,
although I know it's mostly
cellphones, flat screens, razor
wire, beer, and what they call
long guns. *Lubdub. Lubdub.*
So I take a pill, like a good citizen.

Men Walking on the Moon

We were remembering the night in 1969
how young we were, how blue the TV screens,

when someone said it was the only time
she ever heard her father talk about the war.

The good war, ended years before a man
walked on the moon. We turned our faces,

candlelit, toward her. She said that when
he saw the first man's footprint deep

in lunar dust, saw how the tread had stamped
its pattern clean and hard into the soft

white surface and nothing stirred,
he shook his head and said,

That's what the ground was like at Nagasaki
when we were sent in afterward.

Our boot prints sank in ash.
And that was all he ever said of it.

Room Tone

Each body's presence alters the silence
so no one may leave until the soundman says so.
For twenty seconds he wants nothing of us.
Only that we not be the action, the breath, the story,
not stir the particular air of this particular room.
Painful, such necessary stillness.
How our restless histories rise up, batter
the throat's confessional.
The whole business takes forever.
Someone always coughs or cracks a knuckle,
shifts weight heel to toe, a sleeve inside a jacket
rustles and we must begin again
until our smallest human gestures,
tilt of head, finger held to lips, fall away.
We try to be only body, only mass,
unplayed piano, unstruck bow, rectangle
of amber rosin gleaming in a bamboo box.
What frauds we are, how ridiculous our lies,
how deep and wide our neediness,
bellows the din inside our heads.
Our ears fill with hum. Headphones on,
eyes closed, the soundman looks skyward.
We become armchair, bowtie, floorboard, cello, shoe.
We become only what the air plays through.

Oceanic Moment Outside
a Discount Superstore

You never know where likeness lives.
—Elaine De Kooning

The face of Jesus floats atop a swirl
    of motor oil, clouds morph
        giraffe to trombone into snake
and someone else is living
        your exact same life—

      same town, same
shopping center parking lot,
    same semi-reliable car

      like the one you sat inside today,
reusable shopping bag
        of borax, batteries,
      ginger snaps, and soup cans
slung beside you on the seat,
      hands frozen on the wheel, thinking

    this seems odd

until the hot, startled
        breath of someone else's
massive, big-jawed
    dog behind you
      steamed your right ear,
sent you scrambling
      for handle, door,

stumbling out
     onto the blacktop's freshly painted
         lines of demarcation

heart churning hard with the knowledge
     you've once again been served
         the whole thing
upside down and backwards,
     being magnetized to earth's hot core
         and spun hard night and day,
the way we are,

         and there is only likeness
in between us—minuscule
     variations of genetic code
         a billionth of a dust speck
in the empty super-sized
         department store of difference,

making boundary edges clear: how hard
     the manufactured
         surfaces of world
can be against how soft
         our bodies are

how pervious and shifting,
     as we drift past each other

         waiting, walking, held down, splayed out
on asphalt, skin skinned
         away, hands bloody,

blue oil in a pool of water, windblown
        to a Buddha, then a sun, a moon,

or any one of us
        interchangeable as cloud.

Already

this is not what you thought you would be reading
and honestly it's not what I thought I would be writing

either, so quickly everything turns on a word or thought
and we become lost, but this makes us allies now, companions

in an unknown landscape, like students moved midyear
to a new school— cue up the cafeteria humiliation reel,

fire the cheek's fierce burn, those red-hot sparks pocking
holes in the tiny hope chests tucked inside our preteen

hearts and most of us are still packing some of that
sorrow. Whatever story we thought this might be singing

with its words has now slunk down at the loser table
to foot funk level in its plastic seat with corroded chair legs,

or better yet, it turned tail and ran before even walking into
the room like we wish we had done instead of trying to sashay

across the page in the wrong clothes covered with the cheap
perfume of *fake it till you make it* like it's the kind of story

that never sat alone at a table pretending it didn't want to die,
but that story and that story's lie is long gone. So we begin

again. Each day. And look, whatever it was that we didn't
think this would be has been taking shape beneath our noses

this whole time, kneading its own dough, punching it down,
letting it rise, checking the oven, and now warm brown loaves

cool on a windowsill like in a book of fairy tales, curls
of steam lifting from their dark aromatic crusts, delicious,

whole wheat, gluten-free, or however you need it, bread
to pass between us in a story we didn't even know would have

a kitchen or windowsill or cupboard where you find butter
and I find strawberry preserves, or a table where we sit down

together, take out our hidden knives, use them to spread
the slices, smooth the sweet jam, share the bread.

Pantomime

I watch a fat apricot moon
rise through a hotel window in a foreign-to-me town
and burn across a lake above the steep slope

of a volcano's perfect snow-capped cone
and because I am alone

I can't help but wave to another woman
who stops on the walk outside to watch the same
postcard show. She waves back.

I jab my finger wildly at the rising moon
and she nods and jabs her finger wildly at it too

which makes us both tip back our heads to laugh
a laughter that the other cannot hear
which makes us both laugh more

and then, because this moon
is throwing down its molten river almost to the shore

we break into an oddball cha-cha
with each other, impromptu,
through distance and through glass.

We laugh again, our hands and faces to the sky.
Then nod and wave goodbye.

Ode to Customer Support

Oh, human voice on the telephone!
Oh, human voice in a human throat
answering my call for technical support,
my plea for reconsideration
of denied medical bills,
I swear, dear voice: I love you.
Even though you've lied to me.
Even though I know the name
you give is not your name,
even though you know
much more about me than you
say you do, but I don't care.
Breath vibrates along your
vocal chords, you chew
and swallow and you look up
protocols I need, you talk me
through each step, make magic
objects function once again,
almost precisely as their warranties
implied. And once, dear human
voice, during the worst year,
your ear heard panic choke
my throat and you called me *baby*,
told me *not to worry*,
told me *we will work this out*,
your voice a place with wings
I sheltered underneath
while you miraculously
adjusted my bill.

Oh, you gods of account history!
You goddesses of ritual repetition
of identifying information!
Oh, voice of Cedar Rapids,
Bangalore, Toronto, Baton Rouge!
I wish you quiet nights and raucous
bone-deep horn solos, ecstatic
morning glories tumbling from
your garden pots, great sex, great food,
long friendship, and a human voice
answering your cries for help,
all the days and nights of your time off.

3

Object Lesson in Over-Attachment to Outcomes

That's me. I'm like my dog.
My full-bred mutt this bright cold day

sharp black against fresh snow,
nose down, hyena hunched,
ruff high and full out following

the scent of *fox fox fox,*
her dash and gallop frantic

for the musky funk of clever
packed like liquid copper
into black-tipped fur,

fox fox fox fox, whiff after whiff
hard on the track, losing it,

finding it, losing it, doubling back,
disfiguring with desperate
want and fat footpads

the perfect delicate prints
filled to the brim with deliciousness,

my dog and me, how thoroughly
we muck clean trails
with our own needy stink.

Epistemology in the Bathtub in January

A fat fly hatched to life in a harsh month grumbles
      between steamed-up bathroom mirror, white sink,
and this winter rattled window sash I lie beneath,

      sunk gloriously to my neck in hot baby-oiled water
reading aloud to wind gusts whuffing the panes, banging
      the shutter we only last week screwed back

onto the house because who has the time? The poet
      I'm reading listens to lots of music in his poems,
which reminds me to listen to more music

      because when my children were young
all I wanted sometimes was silence, long stretches of silence,
      or deep ocean sound like a gigantic heart

beating only for me. The fly batters the mirror as I read,
      sings its body against it. Perhaps it sees a thousand
flies charging out of that flat misty landscape, a sudden

      climactic battle in a big budget war film, and on cue,
I hear a melody, a *plink plink plink,* played inside
      the glass harp of a water tumbler left on the sink.

The notes repeat, *plink plink* then stop. Song over.
      Mirror empty. The fly has fallen hard for the water
at the bottom of the glass, begun to drown.

This whole next part is silent. I might have
closed my eyes, I might have slipped beneath the steamy water,
    but I only knew the song was panic

once it stopped. That's how this works: you do not
    know a thing, and then, you do.
Wind dies, begins again. Sometimes, it also sings.

Gathering Black Locust Blooms

The edible blossoms
strip so easily
from soft clusters
at your touch
you'd think falling
into your cupped hands
had always been
their plan, how
they mark their
sweetest honey
with deepest color
in their pink throats
precisely where each
fragrant bloom slipped
from its stem.
Strip them gently
straight down
into a brown paper
gathering bag
and leave the bag
open, outside,
for an hour,
to allow spiders
tucked inside petal silk
time to escape.
Oh, you didn't think
there was a catch?
There's always a catch.

Advice Column: House Centipedes

Q.

In my pristine sink
each morning
inked across
a white field
one or two
illegible words
have risen from
unexcavated
cracks that branch
below my house
as though accusing me
of small mean deeds
done years ago
I can't recall
but don't belong
to me I swear
except these damp
weird shames rise up
half-fish, half-beast
with lasso feelers
eyelash legs
so I erase them
into smudges
with a tissue
and pretend that
they were never
there. Oh, god,
what have I done?

A.

Try reading
something other
than your self
for once.
You're not
as awful
as you think.
Nor are they.
Read how those
terrifying squirmy
lines eat aphids,
bedbugs, silverfish
and leave behind
no web, no nest,
no ruined crossbeams,
insulation, no beads
of scat across the floor.
Read how you
can misread
every single thing
and smudge
it with your
humanness.
Next time: try
looking through
a compound eye.

Bird Time

To raise a bird that's fallen
from the nest takes time
but not much time—
                    a minute

from the scattered crumbs
of every hour
for two weeks

        so all together
half-a-morning if you care
to add things up that way.

A small shoe box
of time.

Torn strips of old news
feathering its cardboard floor.

The hard part
is the willingness to push
your finger and a bit
of water-softened brown bread
deep down that screeching
pink-streaked, yellow-throated
need,until the nestling's
strong enough to fly away.

Afterwards, all birds
will seem to sing
a separate song to you.
For years.
But you'll never know for sure.

This Horse

after *Horse,* a cyanotype in sixteen panels by Carrie Witherell

Its white bones float
on blue, its meat a ghost
around the bones, an afterimage
pegged to a wall with silver tacks.

*

Whether the blue is the blue
before dawn or the blue after dusk,
no way to know. Magritte blue,
streetlights on, the tidy houses sharp-peaked.

*

This is a puzzle broken
into sixteen squares.

*

What frightens me: galactic emptiness
in the blank eye socket, the awkward articulation
of those anklebones.

*

Oh, memory of my girl body wrapped tight around the body of a horse!
Hoof beat, heart drum, field, crushed mint, and wind!
Oh, speed and power and heat between my legs
before that has another meaning.

*

All girls have a horsey phase, the Freudians say.

*

I say all skeletons are spectacles.
By which I mean they startle, fill our living bones
with tiny bits of light, exploding.

*

In the bottom of an abandoned silo I found
the skeleton of a cat, curled into a wreath
around its own solitary death.

*

What I don't want to talk about: the relics.
The men on horseback and their statues everywhere.
The lifted hoof, the cape and sword, the bronze.

*

The glue plant either. Or how cities
used to stink of decomposing horse.
Gutter, ditch, and gully.

*

Back, back, back, back to grassy breath and nose,
curry comb following a curve of flank,
to water sucked from bucket and creek,

back to the days when I lay like a blanket draped
across a horse's back, back to the animal
without the bit in its mouth,
the animal, the girl, back, back.
How they nicker through nostril and throat.
How they scare for life.
How they remember.

*

Also: when a horse steps on your foot, it isn't a mistake.

*

Sorrel, chestnut, palomino, gray, roan, cream, black, dappled,
pinto, blaze.

*

I shut my ears to the scientific name for horse, or girl, or blue, or gone.
I chant their colors, turn the hall that holds this horse on end
and place this horse up in the sky,
not winged or mythical,
but standing still.

*

Of every bone I make a star.
Hand flat, I offer sugar to the giant mouth.

Tableau Vivant After Rain

Two enormous gray-white clouds
are reenacting Michelangelo's *The Creation of Adam*

painted on the ceiling of the Sistine Chapel
(which I've only seen in books)

as they drift majestically across
a scrubbed clean sky (its blue, the blue

exclusively reserved for holy raiment), both clouds
maintaining a tense distance between

the fingertips of god and man, incredibly,
this entire time. A miracle, of sorts.

Now, a dandelion puff of cloud on Adam's side
breaks off, lifted by enlightenment

perhaps, or his own (parenthetical) thought.
God and the angels stall. Everyone drifts apart.

Still Life with Your Voice in My Head

First, peach, then knife,
then glints of ebony

guitar, those undulating
umber lines,

hip, shoulder, waist.
The knife's a mirror fixed

to polished bone, the peach
all carmine blush

and cleft—but that guitar's
defying rules,

demanding to be strummed.
A play for time

you whisper in my ear,
even as you break

the rules of silence
made by death,

a ploy to keep the peach
uncut, the knife

blade blameless. You say
it's a conspiracy

of pigment bound in egg
and linseed oil

to hold at bay
deep darkness in the frame.

I say it's working.
Sound a note. And stay.

Unnamed Statue in an Unnamed Church

Unpolished stone, he stands behind
the pulpit's hard curved staircase,
head tonsured, his rough back
to the treads rising toward heaven,
hands outstretched, oil-shined,
grimed by centuries of human touch.
No nimbus, no miter to convey status.
If a saint, he was a minor one.
Carved robe holding equal measures
of light and dark, stone eyes fixed
on some medieval distance, so it
must be the way his blackened ear
tips down toward the living, close
enough for anyone to whisper
ugly truths into it, that drew me
to stand before him, as generations
before me had done, his auricle
scorched with rage and greasy candle
smoke, sooted, stained by what it heard.
Even back then, he must have seemed
an awful miracle: a clergyman who listened,
whose hands offered nothing
and stayed exactly where they were.

My Other Lives Consider the Past

My other lives showed up last night, impromptu.
No one knew exactly who

pitched the idea but everyone gathered,
played darts over beers although a few

of us chose wine or coffee and you-know-who
drank only lemon water with no ice.

She hit the bulls-eye twice.
Then my other lives stepped outside, settled

along the stone wall, dangled legs,
watched the night sky spin above

the fixed points of themselves.
Forgiveness came up, the idea

a fine mist gentling the night,
but an argument broke out over

what happened when and who chose what,
which cracked wide old divides

and launched stirring speeches based on
faulty memory and intangible evidence.

Followed by silence.
Followed by more silence.

Followed by that oh-so-soft
but solid sound a lie

told to no one but the self makes
when it falls like a smooth stone

dropped into a well. My other lives
felt it as it fell

into the still pool
of each self. The evening ended then.

Most of them wandered off to find a bed,
one passed out in the grass,

but the core remained, just two of them,
on lawn chairs, wrapped in quilts,

looking over a small field
as though it were as much of the past

as they or anyone could agree on.
How its grassy weathered undulations

gather up each bead of dewy
condensation, seep of hidden aquifer, and feed

a twisting creek that forks and joins
and twines into a hundred different streams

before it finds the sea.
And that seemed fair to me.

A Cartography of Home

My mother was a place. She was the where
from which I rose. Once on my feet, I touched

my forehead to her knee, then thigh, then hip,
waist, shoulder as I grew into my own wild country,

borderless, then bordered, bound
by terrors, terra incognita and salt seas.

I took my compass rose from her, my cardinal points,
embodiments of wind and names of cloud,

but every symbol in the legend now
belongs to me—rivers, topographic lines and shading,

back roads, city streets, highway lanes that end
abruptly at the broken edge of cliffs

where dragons snorting fire
ride curls of figured waves in unknown seas.

Monsters mark the desert blanks on her charts too.
Before she died, I folded myself back

to pocket-size, my children tucked inside
like inset maps and I lay my head down on her lap.

My mother stroked my hair
the way her mother had stroked hers,

and hers before hers, on and on, and we
remained like that—not long—but long enough

to make an atlas of us, perfect bound,
while she was still a place and so was I.

4

Navigational Notes

What can we do to bring the ship near to its longing?
—Rene Char

1.

Move the longing toward the ship.

2.

Diffuse the gravitational pull and heft
of longing by pretending
there is no longing.
This quiets its sharp-tipped pain,
dulls those mournful cello notes

3.

Call longing by another name—
weakness, witchcraft, turpitude,
dirty-bird-soiling-the-nest, ungrateful child.

4.

Belittle it gently.

5.

Or dominate, humiliate it,
so that longing becomes revulsion
and the ship turns away gladly
from its no-longer-called-longing
even though the ship has not moved
nor the longing
only the names we call things,
the weight and number of stones we have eaten
to steady the ship.

6.

Why *is* the ship not moving?

7.

Why is it anchored and to what?

8.

If those questions are too large
then so is the ship.

9.

Get a smaller ship.

10.

Strip and jump in, swim.

11.

No, don't. Don't strip and swim.
Unknown waters, unknown distances, and longing
that can't find its real name anymore—
too deep, too cold, too blind.

12.

So go in dreams.

13.

Paddle a slim canoe through a moonless night
beneath stars that rise and set
bright in salt water. Trail galaxies
of bioluminescent creatures
in your silent wake
until the curved bow of your boat

nudges a curved shore.
Lean back, watch the turning
stars until everything comes close
and the ship and its longing are one.

14.

Watch for that sky wherever you are.
Watch for that sky.

Enough

Even on cold spring days
when downpours churn the currents
into muddy roils

                the creek turns hard
        exactly where it's always turned

even as it pounds a shoulder
heavy with storm water's weight
against this stream bank

        something unseen in the earth
            refuses to give way.

Not much, but it's enough
to steady me today.

Standard Conditions on Earth

Here, one kilogram is equal to 9.8 Newtons
and when 1.6 million people protest in the streets

of Santiago, Chile, spray-painted slogans bloom
across each storefront, brightly tarting up

the thick dust of a nine-year-drought.
We calculate standard pressure at sea level;

standard temperature at zero Celsius. Neither
can be seen, just measured, just endured,

as though to know how much, how long, how
frequently, might comfort us, and so we plant

our snappy flags and banners marking here
from there. Cold-stunned iguanas drop from trees

when temperatures fall near freezing,
whatever scale one uses, and those poor lizards

never see it coming, which seems funny to us,
the-stunned-and-falling-out-of-trees part, the way

all slapstick gags are funny so long as they're
not us. That's standard too. Besides, just try

to ponder how much happens while we sleep.
Massive ice sheets break away, locusts chew

through miles of millet fields in Kenya, cracks
splinter dams, rust eats through steel,

erasure, birth, mutation, death, tornados,
my neighbor's memory gone overnight

of how spectacular sunsets and sunrises were
when the blast furnaces of Bethlehem, PA,

last smelted iron. Or that he ever told me so.
Or how I see some variation of his vanished memory

now, outside my window, as this scarlet morning
explodes in argument with crimson, orange,

fire-engine-red, which means I'm looking at the end
of the visible spectrum—its measured wavelengths

standardly interpreted as warning, danger, something
particulate ghosting the air we're spinning through.

Standard to try to measure how much dust
what's disappeared kicks up. Standard too, for us

to try to make a song of it, both lullaby and ballad,
a thing to sing and sing and sing until we drop.

Who Can Say

what stretched outside that window//sea or swamp or alto-cumulus cloud shifting//like a North Atlantic fog bank and whether//this was seen through the dark of dream or memory//was a shifting question too until the ruthless//mind's authority stepped in demanding names//Do you agree that cabbage is a funny word//both odd and humorous? The mind//demanded definition and the eye replied//a massive field of cabbages in the dreamy trance//of oceanic moonlight endlessly outside the window//whether dream or memory there is no nailing//any of it down no matter how forcibly the mind attempts//to jack the body up against a wall.//So, more specifics, more detail?//Compact bitter-sweetness packed in pale green//brocade folds around a silky brainstem core.//Times the horizon. Times eternity.//Let's agree it was an endless field of moonlit cabbages//entire worlds coiled inside each one//and whether dream or memory//now there is a field of them inside me too.

Evening View with Turkey Vulture

His pals are hunkered in the sycamore
close by a freshly flattened raccoon carcass,

garnet ribbon of guts greasing the road,
                          but he sits apart, aloof,

on the swamp willow's broken top branch.
Perhaps he doesn't like raccoon.
Or company.

Could be, he's a country store philosopher,
overthinking the gestalt of road and kill,

or a narcissist showing off his dramatic silhouette,

pathologically unaware
that all vultures possess
                the great wings granted to archangels.

Then again, he could be just
another ordinary working stiff

cathartes aura
                golden purifier

beak-and-talon-tired
from a long day's taking up of the dead.

The Ones Who Built This House

built it over years
with plumb line and level
room by room
hearth by hearth
stone by stone

east to west
so the pale sickle
hook of a moon sliding
down the night sky

sets low in the frame
of the newest west window
and rises full butterfat cream
through the watery panes
of old sash facing east

which means we can
walk the years forward
or backward from cabin
to field stone to clapboard

one room to another
door frame to door frame
their lintels and jambs
lined up perfectly squared—

as squared as the shining
cut stones on the hill
standing upright like doors
giving way from the rooms
of this house to the next.

Autumn Orchard

Bent by plenty, yellow-gold,
      maroon with blush
            and speckled rust

the seckel pear bows
      bee-filled bells of sugar
            to the ground

where winter, soon
      enough, will finger-comb
            with cold

each single, green-haired grass head
      gray
      and down.

Deepening the Course

I drag a booted heel through
thick creek gravel, dredge a ditch to keep
storm water pouring off a swollen pool
from washing out the lane, then wait
to check my work. The murky stir
sifts down into a sudden galaxy
of tiny eggs—white shine of dots afloat
in separate jellies—appearing briefly
to be blossoms strung among the branches
of the not-yet budded trees above.
But that's a trick of light on water.
How reflection makes mottled rocks
glow gray-gold as a mackerel sky,
makes creek beds shimmer into cloud,
makes every single thing seem both
itself and every other thing at once.
The starry eggs tremble.
A quickened current pulls against
whatever substance holds them to the stones.
They'll wash away, or hatch, or won't.
The creek will close up every mark I make.
But still, I cannot take it back, what I have done.

Bonfire for Long Marriage

We light kerosene soaked newsprint
in three places so the great heap
shoots up high and hot

yet slow enough to give the panicked mice
who've made their houses inside
everything we piled up

time to flee into the open terror of the field.
They don't turn to watch our old year burn,
but that's exactly what we do—

revel as what we've cast into the flames
reveals itself in fire's one last look.
This year's finale is a wicker love seat,

auction-bought our first year,
now blazing like electric wire,
atop a bed of broken doors,

its grid of carmine intersections
glowing neon in the dark,
collapsing to a shattered lace

of long love's consummations.
We cheer each flaring up, each burning
down. We toast another year.

September Corn with Doves

Curled at the edges, long leaves
bent into broken arms and elbows
jutting out from upright spines,
the cornfield murmurs, rustles,
an awkward graduating class
that shifts and whispers, ears split
open, dry shocks already showing
mouths fat with yellow teeth.
Panicked doves shatter the air
with wing beat, catapult their soft
gray bodies through desiccated
silk and tassel, fleeing an architecture
that won't exist next week when
the combine rumbles through to reap,
thresh, winnow. We startle, leap—
dogs, birds, me. It's the season.
We're not accustomed to it yet.
How quickly whole worlds end.

After Hard Frost

Dead runners from dead pole beans
twist around spade and fork,
cling to boot and tool and root
as I dig this garden under.

I unsheathe a sharp blade,
cut myself free.

Nothing left but habit
and a vine's
tenacious emptiness.

I admit, I also fear the end.
Or maybe not the end

so much as just how hard
I, too, will try to hold on.

Making Hay

Warmth returns, day before least light of the year,
      the field's topography ghost gray
with humped and frost-slumped

      grasses until sunlight stretches down
to kindle prism sparks that glint
      as they're translated into water,

mist, and now, that warmth slips through
      window panes still smudged
with dusty rain, slides over floorboards, shimmers

      up my legs with its sly tongue
of far off sun that lies and lies and swears
      this warmth is back and here to stay.

It's not. Real dark, real cold, are hand in hand
      and surely on the way.
But I've lived this turning tease of seasons

      long enough to push aside both calendar
and clock, stretch out my momentary body,
      meet this momentary touch.

Why We Do It

A young hawk trapped in the barn flies
beam to beam above us, panicked, striking
at strings of daylight between board slats,
but we know to let him be, let instinct

have its way. Escape is down and through
the barn's wide mouth and from the upper rafters
where he rests, his eyes see only solid
threshing floor below. We wait. We wait two days,

two nights. We leave lights on outside
to show the way but he doesn't know
the wild shot chances living forces us to take.
Still, that's not why we hoist a ladder

from floor to loft and loft to peak, not why
we climb up, cut through wire, board, pry open
an old vent and peel it back, not why we climb
back down to wait again. It's not for mercy,

although we hope for it, and not because
we fear discovering his body where it drops
although we think about that too.
The hawk flies past the ragged opening

we've made, turns back, lights on its broken
edge—and then he's gone.
That's why. We do it for that moment
just before he flies—when he sees open sky.

Small Song for Waking in Winter

When he rises first, steps downstairs
     softly in darkness to stir up the fire, start coffee,

and the dog, who's slept heavy as my dead
     across the end of the bed, rises and follows,

when both cats uncoil from their corners,
     rev their small engines to follow

the dog and the man because being cats
     they must know every action,

then I slide my whole body to the bed's exact center,
     stretch into an octopus, sea star,

Leonardo's Vitruvian woman or man,
     until with my backbone, I discover the ridge

between valleys two bodies make in a bed
     no matter how hard they try

to be one. No matter the mattress, no matter
     the love, no matter the years.

I lie still as long as I can, pinned straight through
     the heart by gravity and luck

to this bed in this room in these trees by a creek,
     night sky turning once more to day.

Acknowledgments

My thanks to the editors of the following publications in which some of the poems in this collection first appeared, sometimes in altered form.

About Place Journal: "Inhabitants"

Beloit Poetry Journal: "Room Tone"

Chautauqua: "Why We Do It"

Cider Press Review: "Morning Drift," "Small Poem for Waking in Winter"

Cortland Review: "Kitchen Table"

Lake Effect: "Standard Conditions on Earth"

The Museum of Americana: "Dirt Smart"

Pedestal: "Deepening the Course," "This Horse"

Philadelphia Stories: "Already," "Locks"

Plainsongs: "Men Walking on the Moon"

Poet Lore: "That Summer"

Radar: "Cold Morning with New Catastrophes"

Rattle: "Object Lesson in Over-Attachment to Outcomes"

Red Wheelbarrow: "Speech"

RHINO: "I'm Also the Fox"

River Heron Review: "Epistemology in the Bathtub in January"

Schuylkill Valley Journal: "Pantomime"

San Pedro River Review: "Autumn Orchard," "September Corn with Doves"

Southern Poetry Review: "Still Life with Your Voice in My Head"

Tar River Poetry: "A Brief History of Now," "Enough"

32 Poems: "Liminal," "What We Make Looks Just Like Us"

Thrush: "Navigational Notes"

U.S. 1 Worksheets: "After Hard Frost," "My Other Lives Consider the Past," "Unnamed Statue in an Unnamed Church"

Vox Populi: "After the Press Conference"

I am grateful to so many in innumerable ways. My gratitude to the poetry communities of Bucks and Montgomery Counties for their deep and wide support and to Christopher Bursk whose generosity can never be measured. Big thanks to my No River Twice compatriots, to the Montco Wordshop, and to the Pinkers for inspiration, joy in revision, and friendship. And my thanks to Diane Lockward for her commitment to poets and her clear editorial eye.

About the Author

Hayden Saunier is the author of the poetry collections *How to Wear This Body, Say Luck, Tips for Domestic Travel*, and a chapbook, *Field Trip to the Underworld*. Her work has been awarded the Pablo Neruda Prize, the *Rattle* Poetry Prize, and the Gell Poetry Award, and has been published in numerous journals, including *Beloit Poetry Journal, Smartish Pace, Tar River Poetry, Virginia Quarterly Review*, and *Vox Populi*. Her work has also been featured on *Poetry Daily* and *The Writer's Almanac*. A professional actor, she is the founder/director of the poetry and improvisation performance group, No River Twice, which creates interactive, audience directed poetry readings. She lives on a farm in Pennsylvania.

Printed in the USA
CPSIA information can be obtained
at www.ICGtesting.com
LVHW091921151123
764035LV00004B/439